Awakening to Beauty
Through
Menopause

Susan Winecki

Henschel
HAUS
publishing, inc.
Milwaukee, Wisconsin

Published by
HenschelHAUS Publishing, Inc.
Milwaukee, Wisconsin
www.henschelHAUSbooks.com

ISBN: 979-8-9912791-0-9
LCCN: 2024945527

Printed in the United States of America

Dedicated to women
whose arc is long and mighty ...

Your beauty –

      capsizes, baptizes, rhapsodizes me

unrelenting, unrepenting, fierce, capricious,

    contagious You

      calling me, willing me

        to breathe you, birth you, wild you

              til I am You.

Clad in your voluptuous wetness,

    you spread your watery limbs

wide for me to enter and be graced.

Lake Michigan, Lady Michigan

    I bow to you.

Introduction

These bodies of ours breathe us, feel us, dream us, sleep us, live us, die us.

Miracles ... Mysteries ... We are.

Menopause, the pause that ends our bloodletting—Miracle and Mystery.

Menopause.

A Sacred Rite of Passage in every woman's life.

It's our call to Freedom, which beckons us to claim and honor our wisdom and power, a transition from the Summer of our bodies to the Autumn. Each one of us has her own story. Mine was a heart-awakening experience that became transformational.

The following pages are my Menopausal story. I was blindsided by it, befriended by a rescue dog from the Milwaukee Humane Society and lured by beauty into a passionate love affair with a most unlikely suitor—Lake Michigan. It wasn't love at first sight; just the opposite. Kicking and screaming, I began this journey.

Menopause is often an auspicious time in a woman's life. For some of us, it can be uneventful, no more than a soft, fleeting breeze on our skin and everything in between, including nothing.

It's not an experience or a word that's part of our everyday public discourse. It lives silently behind closed doors for most of us cloaked in misunderstanding and secrecy. For me, it was alarming, disarming, and emotionally destabilizing. Though frightened, I had to tread cautiously, slowly into and through the carefully guarded chambers where lie untended wounds, regrets, endings, sufferings still echoing. In order to secure some footing in this drama holding me captive, I had to recognize that I was in foreign territory and needed to learn how to listen to and accept what my body was asking from me. I had to change my hearing from my head to my heart.

That's how Beauty and Love rescued me in the forms of Lake Michigan and a dog named Kaley.

Menopause was a reckoning for me. Its onset began in the late 1900s and the full force of my symptoms expressed themselves when I turned 50 in the year 2000. Like a storm that erupts when all the conditions are in place, its consequences can have profound, long-term effects. So it was with my Menopausal journey.

This story is a description of those first few years in which I felt most raw and bewildered. I am now a woman in my late 70s writing about how Menopause changed my life. The one-page musings that follow the narrative were written during a brief time in the beginning of my love affair with Lake Michigan. They were crafted when my dog and I walked daily along the shore of the Lake in Bay View. These thoughts, insights, opened my whole being into a new relationship with the sacredness of nature initiated by the beauty and power of Lake Michigan.

My Story

Bay View, Wisconsin. 1993 to 2005

I lived in a three-story, white wooden house with black shutters across the road from Lake Michigan. It was a long-boned, strong-boned house that stood sturdy against the bellowing, bruising blows of the wind and rain. It sheltered two people who lived within and took refuge inside those walls, for we too were long-boned and strong-boned, used to drama, used to storms.

Outside was a yard with well-planted, aesthetically pleasing foliage and flowers. It presented a sense of order and balance to those passing by. You could look at the two people, my then-husband and me, living inside the house, and imagine the same. We were well-constructed, educated, working in professional fields. He was a business owner and salesperson. I was a psychotherapist working in hospitals and business organizations as a Change Management Consultant.

Each of us had developed personas that worked in the world but weren't working so well at home. He was drinking too much and hanging out with friends too often. I was in a period of waiting—waiting for him to change. I felt a deep sense of missing, yearning for what I didn't know at the time.

I could easily say it was him I was missing and waiting for. Part of that would be true, but I had a change to experience that was mine alone and still in shadow at this time. I had become more isolated from family and friends than I wanted to admit. I felt alone and anxious inside but excellent at hiding it.

With a personality well crafted, I cruised through life wearing it. I was tall, smart, sassy, and strong-willed. These traits helped me navigate into and through unsettling and difficult situations, but cracks began to form in my well-crafted self.

It began with tears, accompanied by confusion, uncertainty. Tiny tears, unprovoked soft tears would appear at odd times. It might be a particular thought, driving down a street unfamiliar to me, someone's smile, a rose bush I passed on a walk. I'd find myself tearing up and wondered what was going on. My strong, well-defended persona didn't allow easy tears. I was used to withstanding emotional dramas of every kind.

I grew up in a family with a hard-drinking dad, a hard-working, indominable mother and four older brothers, three of whom joined the Marines after high school graduation. My husband was the second of three brothers and used to drama. His dad had frequent angry outbursts in which all three of them ran for cover.

Between us, there was a surplus of masculine energy with a strong need to stay in control, often by controlling others.

Tears meant vulnerability, weakness, and defensiveness to me. I kept those parts of me hidden. Yet this sudden emergence of tears awakening in me flowed past my defenses. They became a mass of trigger points inside me. It was embarrassing at times. I felt naked emotionally and wondered what was happening, shifting inside of me. *Where was this water coming from?*

Meanwhile, the two of us, ten years married, living inside that white house, were stuck. Neither of us wanted to leave or stay; but there we were, in a limbo of our own making. We weren't willing to give up control and be honest about what was going on in us or between us. That level of vulnerability and honesty at this time was too threatening. Instead, we just withdrew into our own corners which, of course, made the loneliness we felt even more intense.

We had been here before in our years together and one of the ways to get past this chasm was to leave town, go on a trip. Something about a change of scenery, a departure from the dailyness and pressures of our current situation enabled us to step into a different reality for a while.

We could agree on this, so we booked a trip to explore the Mexican Copper Canyon, somewhere we both wanted to experience. We traveled easily together especially when things were rough between us. It seemed like a perfect escape time until we got there and had to reckon with an entirely new set of circumstances that took us both by surprise.

I was lying next to a resort pool before our train tickets would take us to our destination in Copper Canyon. Suddenly, my heart began racing, like it would drive right through my chest. We were both alarmed. After what seemed forever, my heart calmed down but we were in a state of alarm and decided to cancel the rest of our trip. We flew home to get my health checked out.

My diagnosis was not a sudden heart attack but a hormonal fluctuation, not an atypical symptom of Menopause. First the tears coming out of nowhere and now my heart. My husband and I made a truce with each other, in which we agreed to ride out the challenging time we were in for the time being. Neither of us had the energy to make any major relational changes at this juncture.

Since I was in my early fifties, I knew I was coming to that time in my life when midlife transition and Menopause begin to assert themselves. I had had easy menses and assumed that I'd slide through both changes without too much ado. I was well briefed in endings and new beginnings from my work as an Organizational Change Agent.

In that role, I provided facilitator and coaching services to employees who were moving through the onslaught of changes occurring in their workplaces, from downsizing, rightsizing, to sudden lay-offs that resulted in confusion, anger, fear, anxiety. These changes overwhelmed many of them on an emotional level, which was difficult to manage in a corporate setting. In too many workplaces, feelings and emotions, if even acknowledged, are valued little.

In addition, I had experience and skills as a psychotherapist in dealing with life changes accompanied by the volatility and feelings that are intrinsically part of them. I was there to support them in moving into and through this turbulent period in their lives. I helped them create a way to look at and move through these changes in a supportive, forthright and pro-active process. A river was my metaphor for change, which I used in our work by prefacing it with an old African saying, "If you want to get to the other side of the river, you have to get wet."

In essence, you must leave the security and dryness of the riverbank you are standing on and step into the fear and discomfort of the river in order to get to the other side. There are no short cuts. From dry to wet, from security to the unknown, from resistance to action, from fear to courage. Our sessions pulsated with energy as participants saw themselves as actors in this real-life drama. My goal was to facilitate their moving into this transition so it would become transformational for them. They had to face the changes head-on, do their grieving for the parts of themselves and their work lives they had to leave behind, and open new parts of themselves in order to get to the other bank of the river.

Unfortunately, the need for professional services like mine was temporary. Employers would only understand and fund their employees' stresses and traumas for a limited time until they began to close the doors to outside vendors such as me. I found myself in the middle of my own work ending in the area of expertise I cherished and had developed many skills in. Now it was time for me to make changes in myself and my life. My own riverbank was collapsing beneath me, and I had to recognize that I too was in the river of change and needed to cross to the other side.

Susan Winecki

~ ~ ~ ~ ~ ~ ~ ~

Change is a thief, a body snatcher, a heart breaker

    it takes from us the ones we love most

Change is an ax murderer, cold-blooded, merciless

    dreams, jobs, homes, futures...non-discriminating

Change is a life-giver, a dawn bringer, a shape shifter

    an energy wild, wise, ancient, primal

Change is a master of disguise. We love it, hate it, crave it, resist it, our bane and balm can it be anything less than holy?

~ ~ ~ ~ ~ ~ ~ ~

I had participated in a monthly Dream Group for many years at that time. Facilitated by a Jungian Analyst, we came together to share different perspectives and thoughts on the dream being presented. I knew the significance of dreams, especially when they are vividly remembered upon awakening and a recurrent thread runs through them.

During this time of inner confusion and turmoil, I had three dreams in a row, each with a similar theme cloaked in different circumstances. In the first one, I wandered barefoot through a strange terrain, lost and frightened. I was supposed to be doing a presentation for a work group and had no idea where I was or how to get to where I was supposed to be.

In the second dream, I was in front of an audience about to make a presentation and I completely forgot my words and had no written remarks to refer to.

The third dream was a repeat of the second with some variation. Essentially, they reflected my inner states of anxiety and bewilderment and confirmed for me that I was entering a new reality.

My professional work had come to a halt, my marriage was in trouble, and I was an emotional wreck.

A storm was brewing inside of me. It began with tears, then heart palpitations, and now a whole battery of symptoms erupted, including vaginal hemorrhaging, night sweats, hot flashes, skin drying, restlessness, emotional swings. All the classic symptoms of Menopause all at once.

Why?

Why was I being accosted by this band of renegade symptoms? My mom had slid through this change without much ado and my menses were easy. As I talked with other women friends, I learned my symptoms were the worst. A few of them never had a hot flash and didn't know what they felt like.

I wondered how this could be happening to me. I couldn't trust the mystery happening in my own body to be a safe place for me to reside it at this point. I felt this wildness inside with aspects of all parts of myself in disarray, screaming for attention. I had fallen from grace with the external world and found myself thrust into an internal crisis. There seemed to be no escape.

Up until then, I had a whole pattern of life arranged in Mondays, Tuesdays, Saturdays, and it was now in disarray and confusion. One of the hardest parts of this time was giving myself permission to be in it, to be willing to experience fully what was happening inside of me.

What that meant at the time was literally stepping down, stepping away from this professional self I had created and lived through. I told myself and others that I was on sabbatical and needed to figure out where to go from here.

With everything coming to a halt in the outside world, I had time on my hands. Now I was at home, fighting off the legions of demons who taunted me endlessly about what I was doing at home when successful, interesting people were all at work solving problems, making important decisions, changing the world. There were days when I let the demons win and just felt worthless, helpless, and defeated.

Some part of me knew that whatever was going on in me was significant and I needed to stay with it, to get to an understanding of it. My body was in control now, and it frightened me. This was a version of Menopause I was in the dark about.

My usual mode of dealing with unexpected change was head on, stay tough, strong, controlling—not only myself but everyone in the situation. When the storm passed, things would return to normal and that would be that. But somehow, this crisis I was in felt like my usual M.O. wasn't going to work. I had an intuitive sense that whatever was going on in and with me was wanting something I wasn't aware of at this time.

What was going on in me that caused such massive disruption and discomfort? I desperately wanted to understand why I was having such a difficult time with this so-called natural transition in every woman's life. I hit the books, did massive research on menopausal symptoms, sought out alternative remedies that helped to decrease the intensity of my experience.

I wanted to get through it as naturally as possible like so many women before me. This had to be more than a physical manifestation of change, even though that's all that the information I culled told me.

I know from my own experience that every physical symptom of pain or distress that occurs in my body has an emotional and psychological component, an unresolved stress, a loss unexpressed. That's what I wanted to explore now and try looking at it from another perspective.

What if I began to look at Menopause and mid-life transition through a softer lens, like that of moonglow instead of the harsh glare of sunlight? What if I tried accepting this crisis and adjusting to these changing conditions until I had more insight or clarity? This focus enabled my symptoms to decrease a bit in intensity, to become more bearable and less intimidating, but only a bit.

My husband's salary enabled me to take this time for myself, so I surrendered to this new reality and moved into a quieter, more introspective place within me. I thought about my work with Change and how frequently, when I asked clients who were having an easier time adjusting to the workplace endings and shifts, what enabled them to move through the process more readily?

Some said their Faith helped them cope and come to terms with the drama of the upsets. Faith. It rooted and held them in place when the floodgates of change opened. Faith. Where was mine? Something to think about as I settled into silence.

I began journaling, meditating regularly, praying for guidance and clarity in this period in which I had time on my hands. My husband had a business to run and that's where his energy was invested. I was on my own.

I turned my attention to thinking about this experience through an exploration of Faith and what that meant to me personally. I'd always been a seeker, traveling different spiritual paths. Growing up Catholic, moving through a series of spiritual and faith-based traditions, including rituals and ceremonies in Ancient Goddess study; a year of Mystery School in New York with Jean Houston; Jungian Analysis and my own personal therapy. I had spent the last several years of study and immersion in Native American Spirituality rituals and ceremonies.

I realized I was missing a faith that had at its core a feminine power and presence. My body was feminine, woman, earth, water, moon. I was carrying and coddling those concepts in my con-sciousness from all those years of study, but I hadn't fully integrated them, hadn't connected them into my own earth body self. Is that what was gestating within me now? Were all those experiences converging in me now?

That led me to more questions about the endings in my own life that didn't serve me any longer; and the coming into being of new parts of myself. How would this experience be more relevant and purposeful if I saw it as a deepening, a ripening of my own spiritual process? What if I allowed my body to experience itself through the full force of the storm within me?

I was in my own river now, wet and wretched, feeling my way thought these dark, uncomfortable waters. I had to get to safety, to the other side of this experience.

As I spent time in my aloneness, my mind swirled with remembering all the empty calories of negative messages I had eaten and stored in my consciousness about *who* I was and *how* I was as a female, as a woman. Endless messages about not being enough or the other side, which was that I was too much. Now those messages were coming untethered, blasting through me like a rock concert. I practiced putting my hand over the mouth of those rock star inner critics when they came taunting with familiar voices of shaming, guilting, should-ing.

I was being challenged to get down to the raw of myself in order to respond to an urgent call from some part/s of me imprisoned, impaled, stuck, screaming for attention through my body. I was in the emergency room of myself, wanting a diagnosis, some kind of affirmation that made sense to me.

Nights were the hardest when the river overflowed its banks and sleep was stingy. I peeled the wet sheets from my body and sat down in night's lap with the moon as my companion and waited, just sat in the waiting, in the silence. Never before had I felt so alone. Like a piece of driftwood floating on an endless sea with no end in sight.

There was nowhere to go, nothing to do but surrender, so I did— again and again—and slowly things began to shift inside of me. I still felt wet and wretched but my body began to let go, relax and become more fluid, like the element whose jaws I was in. As I listened to the pulsing of my heart, to the ebb and flow of my breath I began to feel myself on the inside. maybe for the first time ever.

I was in my body. Everything happening was in my body. My limbs were softening, my skin was softening, my heart was softening. A tenderness was rising inside of me for myself. I had kept myself so tightly wound with busyness and doing for so much of my life, I wasn't even aware of how restrictive, how stiff I had become in my body, in my mind. My whole being had formed into straight lines and sharp corners instead of musical notes.

Now I was becoming more fluid, like the river that I was in, holding me in its embrace. I was the one who needed healing now and the healer in charge was me. I had coached my clients through this treacherous river of change and now I had to coach myself through it. I needed to replace this patchwork of thorns around my heart with patience, empathy, encouragement and love. I had a mountain of understanding and empathy when others needed tending to; I just had too little to none for myself.

The bellowing, barking, the violent uprising of these Menopausual systems were my own wounded, frightened, repressed, and restricted feminine soul/body demanding to be heard, acknowledged, claimed, and loved into being by me. I had to move from my head to my heart.

Certainly, in my years of personal therapy I had covered a lot of ground in my healing process but there's always more. In my growing-up house, my dad bragged about having four sons and two blanks. The "blanks" were my younger sister and me. In his and the world's eyes, we had no status, value, or redeeming qualities. Ironically, my mom was the heavy lifter in our family. Grounded, hard-working, responsible, the iron backbone holding us all together when my dad was happiest away from us, often in taverns. I fought with my dad often and resented his dominant make-believe role in our family, when it was my mom whom we obeyed and respected.

I had a strong awareness of gender inequality from early on and I carried it into the world. I was deeply in need of affection and tenderness I hadn't had growing up. My mom was too busy working full-time while tending to the six of us that she simply wasn't available for the attention and nurturing I yearned for as a sensitive, tender-hearted growing girl.

I wasn't conscious of just how deeply imbedded this missing was in me. I operated with a surplus of masculine head energy to manage and control, which served me well in the workplace and the challenges intrinsic to getting on in the world. The shadow side of the imbalance of my inner masculine and feminine rendered me quick to anger, to defensiveness, to pointing fingers at men for all the problems in the world.

What was now gestating inside of me was a new feminine consciousness that was ancient, alive, and coming up through my body. It wasn't about blaming men; it was about naming and claiming my own feminine power.

From those early formative years, I didn't know that Menopause could be the path to my own deeply buried, sensuous feminine being. I didn't know her name would be Beauty. She was beckoning me, initiating me into a love affair that had waited so long, so patiently, so tenderly. All I knew at this time was that my body was bolting like a wild stallion breaking free of its holdings. Parts of me tucked away in my own deep-earth self were surfacing, breaching, reaching for the light.

In my journaling, in my sitting in the dark of night, feelings of freedom, of wildness would take hold of me and send my imagination soaring with curiosity. I had always been drawn to emotional drama. A steady diet of it in my family, my husband's, and our blended family kept us in an emotional drama loop for much of the time.

But this was different.

These feelings, these arisings, were coming from me to me. I was feeling a new sense of myself, but I had to be vigilant and cautious with what I was feeling. If I thought of this experience as a spiritual crisis, then what do I do with it? A match lit the fire inside me, but where do I go from here?

There was so much at stake in this turning. Do I leave my marriage? What about my work? I no longer had a safety zone. My well-crafted self remained long-boned and strong-boned but the marrow inside was softening. I could see clearly that there was a before and after to my situation. I was growing a new sense of self, but I was far from being ripe enough to leave the branch I was attached to so tenuously. I was frightened to the core. I felt like a slice of ice severed from its glacier home, sent out into a terrifying sea of aloneness without an explanation, without a way home.

I trusted the way my life had worked until now. There was a rhythm I counted on. I met people and opportunities at the time I was ready to move in that direction. My work for several years was with a woman who became a professional partner in providing employee development services in teambuilding, problem-solving, change management.

When we ended our professional partnership to move on separately, I knew that I wanted to specialize in working with employees dealing headfirst with changes they were confronted with at work. I moved seamlessly into that role and loved it. I trusted that whatever I was supposed to be doing next would happen. I was used to making new friends and greeting new experiences.

I attended a Jungian Psychology lecture one Sunday afternoon years ago at the Unitarian Church on Ogden Avenue and a woman next to me in the audience began a conversation with me. I told her about a chance meeting I had with the full moon the night before when it seemed to follow me home as I walked in its light. She invited me to join a Dream Group that had been meeting for several years once a month to share dreams and discuss what their meaning might be. I immediately said yes. I now have been part of the group for over 40 years—an example of synchronicity at work.

But this time was different. I was lost at a crossroads as I tried to understand what to do with these new awakenings. I had no frame of reference for the raw, intense vulnerability I felt. My inner wretchedness led me to a new sensitivity of suffering in others, particularly animals who are caged.

Around this time of my confusion and worry about all the unanswered questions buzzing around inside of me, I dreamed about dogs. They would show up and be part of a larger dream I was having, not playing any major role that I could focus on. I read an article about the Humane Society needing volunteers to help at the local shelter. I had time on my hands, so I took on the role of Adoption Counselor, which meant matching an orphaned dog with a person/s wanting to take one home.

I checked in and walked past cages of needy eyes, paws, and noses pressed against the metal bars. It was heart-wrenching and I wanted to bring all of them home with me.

One dog named Kane drew me in. He had been at the pound for over three months. He didn't approach the cage door when someone walked past, looking for a dog to take home. The other dogs were eager to be looked at and claimed, but he was different.

The information sheet that people fill out said he had been kept in the garage so perhaps he was used to being alone. In quiet times, I would bring him out and spend some time with him. He was a rough cut of a guy, a gangster, kinda like a Marlon Brando personality type—fifty pounds of thick, mostly black-hair with tan and white trim, medium-sized, distrusting energy. I was attracted to his stubborn strength immediately, as I had to use some of my own strength to get him out and into his cage again.

A kind of intuitive sense in me signaled that this dog and I were supposed to meet and companion one another. I brought him home. A total rule-breaker, he forbade our three cats from being on the floor when he was there; chewed shoes, looked for any opportunity to sneak out of the house and whine mightily when brought back in.

My husband wanted me to take him back. I refused. He was mine. He knew it and I knew it. Just knew it. Just felt it. Just trusted it. The moment I leashed him and we headed down to the Lake for our first outing together, he took one look at that blue-fleshed, voluptuous stretch of wet Lake and was a goner.

Lake Michigan cast its spell on him and sent his long-repressed raw, primal instinctual being into high gear as he fought to get off the leash and plunge into it. It took the strength of Hercules to contain him, to keep him tethered and somewhat under control.

How I ever got him away from it on that first day, I'll never know. You read stories about people lifting cars off trapped kids or some other unfathomable feat of strength and that's how I felt pulling him back to the house that first day after his introduction to Lake Michigan.

Once home, Kane, transfixed and mesmerized, would lie on a chair by the window that faced the Lake. He was helplessly, hopelessly, utterly captivated by Lake Michigan's allure. Too wild and undisciplined to walk unchaperoned.

~ ~ ~ ~ ~ ~ ~ ~ ~

50#Wild
Take him back! Get rid of him!
shrews my husband, tracking
a trail of torn shoe remnants
A pound survivor surrendered
after a series of household felonies
he settles in. Dawn trembles
with his high-pitched wailing
desperate to head out into
beckoning dawn
Choking, gasping, pulling
a sled dog in silver clawed noose
bursting into freedom

Nose dripping, fur bristling, eyes on fire
like headlights on the back of
a fast-moving car, we head downhill
round the bend where the blue diamond waits
I pull the trigger, he breaks into ecstasy
a rifle shot racing across stony shore
snapping at white toothed waves until
formless
I stand aroused, heart pounding, nostrils
swollen, hair pressed down by wind
my fire and his....akin
He's running me, breathing me, dripping me
I, too, quicken at the smell of
rotting autumn earth, lusty cries of
gulls on the hunt, ragged edges of
waves on blackened Lake
I watch myself ... wild
That's way he stays.

~ ~ ~ ~ ~ ~ ~ ~ ~ ~

I had lived in Bay View with a view of Lake Michigan since 1993 and acknowledged what a blessing it was to have the Lake in full view from every room in the house. I walked with friends. We engaged in endless chatter about endless, never-ending personal and relational dramas.

The Lake was in my peripheral vision. It's not that I was impervious. I nodded, affirmed and extolled the virtues of the Lake as we walked. Others told me I was fortunate to live so near the Lake yet it remained distant, background. This beautiful and powerful body of water was not an entity I could be intimate with. I remained in a kind of sensory fog for what seemed an eternity. I stayed in polite yet admiring distance from it. People had that place in my life. I hadn't extended myself in friendship with the natural world around me. I lived inside my long-boned walls where I felt safe and transparent.

~ ~ ~ ~ ~ ~ ~ ~ ~

Kane was my dog's name and I renamed him Kaley at this time as Kane sounded too much like the bad son, Cain, in the biblical story of Cain and Able and I didn't like that association. I quickly became his crack-of-dawn daily escort on walks to Lake Michigan. There I was, bleary-eyed, half-dead from insomnia, throwing clothes on, leashing him up, flying across the road, down the hill, around the corner where Lake Michigan lay luxuriantly, like the world's largest blue diamond.

Kaley cared not a lick that I was in a deep, unrelenting personal and soul crisis. At the first eyelash of morning, he was like a comet, ready to go, with me panting behind him in rain, sleet, frigid, humid, in every kind of Wisconsin weather unbearable, we went out to greet the Lake and walk beside it.

I'd never experienced a being as intense, as alive as he was. Every hair on his body quivered with a kind of inner electrical current as we walked. His paws grasped the ground to steel himself steady as he poured himself down the path to the Lake. I followed blindly, obediently, on the other end of his leash, holding on for dear life. He could teach a masterclass on focus and determination.

The two of us leaned into the unfolding morning and became buddies, each dependent on the other for this part of our journeys. He was a no-nonsense, tough teacher, relentless in his struggle to feel his freedom with me holding him back, which I had to do most of the time. He couldn't be trusted on his own. Me neither.

The two of us were becoming uncaged; his from the pound and mine from years of a repressed feminine self, lying in wait for this time and place in which to weave all my broken pieces into a new tapestry. We were on the move, on the hunt for a new kind of freedom; a freedom to be seen; to be heard; to bring some light into the prison we carried within us.

Kaley was an orphan, a whirling dervish, a shaman, who connected me to unknown parts of myself, still dormant. Every now and then when there was no one around, I'd release him from the leash and let him chase the snapping waves on the shoreline. Getting him back on the leash was some kind of miracle.

~ ~ ~ ~ ~ ~ ~ ~ ~ ~

Time melted into itself as Kaley and I walked. It became a ritual, like going to Catholic Mass in the morning as a grade-school kid. As we walked the same path each day, something began to shift inside of me. It was almost imperceptible, so subtle and soft, like a warm fire coming up through my feet, spreading through my limbs, moving into my heart, my eyes.

My feet now pawed the earth, claiming the ground beneath them. My whole body became a sensory feast. What I had looked at and driven by a thousand times, I saw for the first time. No longer separate, no longer walking along the shore in a sensory fog, I began to feel that I was a part of what my eyes and senses beheld.

It was impossible to witness a love affair so passionate and all-consuming as Kaley's with the Lake without it touching me also. I wanted to know what it was about Lake Michigan that Kaley found so alluring. What made him leap with total trust and abandonment into her watery arms? What was the magic in her calling to the magic in him?

I knew I wasn't going to be leaping into that artic-cold water anytime soon, but Kaley forced me to pay attention to what was awakening in me through feeling, seeing, imagining as we walked this path each day. I began to slowly, sensuously show up, and be present; to move into my own love affair with Lake Michigan.

A beautiful being under just the right circumstances can render one breathless and besmirched with little to no effort. Kaley and I were ready and willing to be seduced and who better than beauty in the form of Lake Michigan to seduce us.

And she didn't come alone to our clandestine meetings. She brought the sky, clouds, gulls, and mallards and sun and moon and shadow and light and wind and all the living moving beings within her and around her.

And we brought all of ourselves to her.

The drama that I was so drawn to in my ordinary life was now manifesting in nature. I felt like Sleeping Beauty being aroused from a deep slumber by the kiss of beauty. This body of water that I had looked at and driven by a thousand times, I now saw and felt for the first time. Awe and wonder streamed through my whole self and I was a part of this beauty that I experienced. Right here in my eyes, my hair, my breast, legs and belly but most of all, my heart.

This yearning, woven through my dreaming, underground self was a dreaming for the deeply missed, forgotten intimacy with the earth, with the natural world. Lake Michigan was its stunning centerpiece. I longed to feel part of the larger, wilder, more complex and interesting reality I found myself immersed in.

Once again, the teachings of Native American Spirituality, specifically the Lakota Sioux, came to mind with their central tenet of relatedness. That all sentient beings, are related, interconnected, all part of and sharing in the same mystery and fabric of life. And if that is true, then it is also true that not only did I have a longing to be in deeper relationship with the natural world around me; all the beings in the natural world had a desire to be in relationship with me. Our longing is reciprocal.

The sun comes out to greet me, gets in my eyes, makes me blink and sneeze so I must giggle and say hello. The wind shakes me loose from constricted feelings and thoughts and messes my hair in playfulness. The moon watches over me in the dark of night. The trees stand vigilant and silent as I pass but I see them, and they see me from their own tree-selves.

No longer separate as I walked along the shore looking out, I felt part of the beauty my eyes beheld, part of the beauty that enveloped me. It had seized me somehow and pulled me into itself.

Kaley was no longer rousing me out of bed to begin our pilgrimages to the Lake. I was now easily awakening and running in anticipation alongside of him. Lake Michigan was beckoning, and I was heeding her call. Entering the raw, primal beauty of the elements shrouded in morning tender, my body began to remember itself ancient, wild, summoned by the slapping waves on the shore, the smell of musky earth, the screeching cries of gulls circling the shimmering blue sea of Lake spread voluptuously as far as my eyes could see. And she became a living entity, a spiritual presence and power that enveloped and held me in her liquid embrace.

I was uncoiling from my own dark womb and my inner deadness; I was sprouting new shoots that reached for the light of beauty. I moved toward it, into it. It filled me with grace and curiosity. I wanted to explore this natural, sensuous world of nature awakening in me. Moving into the stark and stunning beauty of the Lake first thing each morning while I was still half-conscious began to thaw me, slowly, steadily like a slow-motion camera that captures the infinitesimal movement of a flower unfolding, petal by petal.

Lake Michigan became a living entity, a spiritual presence and power that reached out to me, softly, quietly. I no longer cared or crowed about the weather as I used to. I was seeing it now as a mirror of my own constantly changing and shifting inner states and moods and becoming more accepting of that in me.

I began to feel a sense, an unusual sense of safety and intimacy in the Lake's presence. I felt held and cherished in ways that I had never experienced with other humans, and my tears responded to the tenderness I felt. Little tears at first and then giant tears. Tears I had been carrying in me my whole life. Tears of childhood hurts, ridicules, exclusions, tears of losses, relationship endings, misunderstands and resentments. They poured out of me, a river, unspoken, unscripted as we walked.

Those tears and their aftermath moistened my imagination and removed the veil from my senses, and I began to feel Lake Michigan and myself with a reverence I had only known in moments of prayer.

Our walks became holy as her beauty beckoned and welcomed us.

One day, I remember turning the corner just as the sun rose from the liquid womb of the Lake, making the slow climb up to his throne. Garlands of color splashed across the sky as he rose. She lay beneath him, covered in diamond rays.

Kaley and I would stop and stand in awe. Sometimes we stepped lightly around the corner if we had gotten an extra early start and we'd be quiet as though she too were just coming into her day, and we didn't want to alarm her with our sudden appearance. Our morning walks were laced with magic and drama.

Susan Winecki

The story of Lake Michigan is an epic one. Born from the melting glaciers some hundred thousand years ago, she was formed in beauty and drama. Walls of crushing stone parted and made space for her to begin her reign as a Great Lake, one of five sisters, including Huron, Ontario, Superior, and Erie, whose territory lies solely within the United States. Her Queendom encompasses Wisconsin, Michigan, Illinois, and Indiana. Her first subjects were the Native American tribes of Menomonee, Sac, Fox, and Potawatomie, who lived and thrived in her presence and bounty for thousands of years until white-skinned settlers seeking land and its riches drove them out of their homes and livelihoods.

These original inhabitants lived simply, abundantly and resourcefully along the shores of this mighty water. They named it Michigama, Great Water. Her body, long and narrow, 307 by 118 miles, teemed with native fish and a wealth of plant and animal species who drank at her feet along with winged ones who soared above her.

Lake Michigan carries the memories and remnants of those ancient beings whose lives interlaced with hers. One can only imagine the beauty and power of Lake Michigan's original face at birth and the deep attachment and love those early earth dwellers had for her. I see her today as chalice, living spiritual vessel who quenches the thirst of forty million people, along with other sentient beings who gather at her side to drink and bathe and cool themselves in the heat of day.

Now, for me, she became chalice, an elegant container of constantly changing beauty and drama, holding a place for me in which to restore my still-delicate self. I saw her as Goddess, Queen, holding court with all her subjects; soaring and swooping gulls, geese; cloud formations, wind currents, moonlight, sunlight, swimming creatures and plants, a morgue for sunken ships. Life and death she carries in her womb, and all are welcome.

Like Kaley alongside me, I too felt hopelessly, helplessly, utterly captivated. And I wanted to be like her—reckless, wildly alive with energy streaming through me. I wanted to be free like her; audacious, independent, refusing to be tamed and tethered for others' comfort and convenience, answering to no one, beholden to no one except the power that coursed through her slick and sensuous body and mine also.

I wanted to be wise and beautiful like her and I was. She told me I was. She whispered to me that she and I were fashioned from the same breath that formed mountains and rainbows and sunsets. If her body is sacred, so was mine. She was birthed to express the liquid element of the Divine and I was made human to do the same—each in our own way and time. She gave her heart to me. I gave mine back to her.

Susan Winecki

~ ~ ~ ~ ~ ~ ~ ~ ~ ~

Lake Michigan

You summon me from
the deep forest of thoughts
beckon me to your blueness
lure me from the lair
of loneliness, cradle me
in your liquid lap
You ripen me
sweeten me
reveal yourself
to the wild sea in me
I empty my heart pockets
make room for you
make love for you
make prayer for you

~ ~ ~ ~ ~ ~ ~ ~ ~ ~

I was crossing the threshold now into new markings like a snake who sheds an old skin at the same time growing a new one. I became a glutton, a connoisseur, a fool for Beauty. It summoned and I surrendered. That is my story.

When those first few years of midlife and Menopause collided with me, I suffered deeply and died, but not for long. I had other parts of me to ripen into being. Beauty bowed me into submission.

Lake Michigan was my initiation. She baptized and blessed me. Most of all, she mirrored for me what was already mine. I was learning this about beauty. When it beckons, it means business. It is willing to remain landscape, background in our lives but there's a price to pay for this veiling. We risk living with closed hearts and silenced souls. There is also risk in unveiling, for it requires the willingness to turn oneself over to the life-loving, soul-awakening power of the earth in order to be reshaped into new markings and curves.

One must make way, time, and love for beauty.

Beauty
The gentle of you brings silence
silence of you brings tears
tears of you bring gratitude
gratitude for you brings
the ineffable

I had a dream while I was writing this piece about an old woman who lived in my neighborhood as a young girl. I hadn't seen or thought about her for over forty years. Her name was Mary, small in stature with warts and gnarled hands and lonely, vacant eyes. Her head was always wrapped in a threadbare toweled turban, and she spoke not a word of English. She lived alone in a brown-shingled decrepit house whose windows were covered with tan paper. My friend and I were sure the house was filled with dead bodies.

We would walk to her house on summer days out of boredom and the need for a little excitement. We'd often find her hoeing her big garden or resting on the stoop of her broken-down porch. We'd harass her and call out her name in a teasing way to get her riled up and she'd chase us and we'd run and scream. It was fun for us to be chased and yelled at by her in her own strange language.

Sometimes my mom would make a sweet that we'd place on Mary's back porch in front of her door. Then we'd hide in the bushes and call her name and before long she'd poke her head out, look around, snatch the dish, and take it inside.

My friend and I did this for a couple of summers. Then we lost interest as kids do when they get older. But during that strange time, we even befriended her. One day, she let us into her house. The one room that she lived in served as a kitchen with an old-fashioned cast-iron cook stove. A bundle of blankets on the floor apparently served as her bed. She had rows of red chili peppers hanging from the rafters. The room was very old and smelly but kind of warm and cozy too.

I dreamt that my friend and I went to the cemetery to dig up her body in the deep of night. By moonlight, we picked up shovels and dug until we unearthed her body. She rose slowly to the surface in a reclining position with dirt falling away in great patches. Her skin was pink and glowing like a young woman's. We fell back in fright, awe and silence, then moved toward her to ask how she could breathe if she was dead, deep in the ground. She said she'd been alive under the earth for a hundred years waiting to be dug up.

That was the dream. It was a prophetic dream, yet personal and collective. It said to me that the feminine soul of the earth was returning, rising, being restored to life and that I was part of the rising.

The dream also affirmed for me that I needed to go to the deep underground of myself to heal the wounds buried and carried for so long inside of me. This feminine spirit, this feminine power, was rising in me just as in my dream and I needed to express how this felt.

When wounds and hurts are named, claimed, held, and rocked in holy healing within us, a new energy is released, made available for our empowerment. Creative energies are intrinsic to our being but often trapped in the prison that our wounds occupy within us.

As we gain access to more of our majestic powers, creativity is unleashed and bristles forth in ways and means only each of us knows in ourselves. For me, the river water that became a flood in Menopause metamorphosed into a flood of words that poured out of me onto paper.

I began writing.

After Kaley and I returned from our walks, I frequently wrote about my thoughts, imaginings and feelings. These writings became "Lake Michigan Musings" that express what I brought with me after spending a precious morning in Lake Michigan's presence. Kaley curled up in his chair and I wrote.

Kaley, my wild, innocent, beloved friend and spiritual matchmaker, rescued me from my inner pound and I rescued him from the outer one. For a time in each of our lives, we companioned and loved one another. Kaley would leap into the blue chair in front of the window facing the Lake and stare at her in a delirious daze of rapture. She tenderized and mellowed him. Not only him, me too. She opened a new creative urgency in me to pay tribute to her thru these musings.

We continued to live in this house in Bay View on the front shore of Lake Michigan until my mom in her nineties came to live with us. Our family lived alongside the Wisconsin River when I was growing up. My mother had a hard time relating to the majesty and vastness of Lake Michigan. She was a river woman who related to the closeness and immediacy of the Wisconsin River, which glided past our house. Around this time, Bay View became very popular with increased traffic, congestion and noise.

It seemed natural to make a move to a quieter place, so we moved to an old house alongside the Milwaukee River.

Kaley died before we moved from Lake Michigan to the river. I carried his ashes on a freezing cold, fourteen-below-zero day with a wind chill of thirty below, down the hill, around the corner, straight to the Lake Michigan shore. The sand and rocks were ice-covered, treacherous. He would have loved it.

Sometimes he would escape from the house, make his way down to the Lake, and return covered in ice from head to foot. I opened the box and removed the plastic bag with his remains with pounding heart and shaky fingers. His release into the wild, thunderous waves was at hand and I let him go. The wind claimed him now on his final run. His ashes leaped out of the bag in two or three great gestures and emptied itself. He was free now.

Lake Michigan lives in my bones, my heart, and spirit. Even though I moved away from the Lake physically, she had transformed my life so I could move. I was ready to begin a new chapter.

I became a hospital chaplain after I completed a Doctoral Degree in Ministry from the University of Creation Spirituality in Oakland, California. My husband I divorced a few years after we moved to the river. We had reached the end of our marital journey together. Both of us had changed and were ready to move on.

My mom moved to Durango, Colorado, to be with my daughter and her family. My husband remained in the house until it sold. I moved back to the Lake in a co-op housing building and now have a lovely view of Lake Michigan from my living room windows.

My dad is dead now and the blanks he called my sister and me have become two competent, healthy, deep-feeling, compassionate women. Lake Michigan was my spiritual anchor and my mid-wife then and now. I still walk and tell her how grateful I am to know and love her and now you can read some of the one-page essays and poems I wrote while in her aura.

I learned from this experience with Menopause that it too, like Lake Michigan, is an epic story and this is the story I leave you with. I am in my late seventies now. I wrote the words that follow while in my fifties. I know that we must claim our woundedness by feeling it, painting it, writing it, speaking it, and dancing it 'til it turns to joy and freedom. These are my parting thoughts about this life-changing, life-deepening experience I have come to think of as "rewombing."

~ ~ ~ ~ ~ ~ ~ ~ ~

Menopause has its own language, just as dreams do, and it behooves us to pay attention to it. If we were more in balance with our body voices and cues, shifting from mental, external energy to more internal, psychological, emotional and spiritual energy, it's likely we would experience less symptomatic issues during this transition. We learn to hold on tightly to this version of ourselves we've been living in for the first part of our lives. We come into this birth, curious, loose-limbed and hungry for life—a huge transition from our mother's watery womb.

As girls, too many of us are fed gallons of, "no, not now, be quiet, sit still, don't touch that, etc." We begin to pull back from our natural buoyancy because it makes people uncomfortable. Too many of us become private, careful persons fearful of offending or making others notice us. We shut down those parts of us that are still alive, craving freedom and that's why Menopause is an auspicious time in our lives; a time of asking our bodies what they want from us.

Our work is to wake up, to become conscious of who we are and what we are doing in our lives to honor and appreciate this consciousness. That would mean being aware and responsive to the messages rippling through us. This process of menopausal awakening and awareness is universal to women, yet every woman has her own unique experience of it. What may be dreadfully uncomfortable for one woman may be hardly noticeable for another.

This demonstrates how unique this rite of passage is for each of us. It's easy to forget that we are natural beings with a natural rhythm that corresponds to the natural order of life on earth. When we work in attentiveness with this life energy, we are happier, healthier, and easier in and with ourselves.

I hated Menopause when I was in the jaws of it, biting down into my flesh, drawing blood that so terrified me. I hated my body feeling the bites, tasting the blood. I didn't know that this was my initiation in a new mystery, that of my own body, my own sensuousness, my own aliveness. I needed to be bit hard, skin-breaking hard, to wake up to that which was mine all along.

Our bodies can change a great deal on the outside of us as well as on the inside during this menopausal migration. For some of us, our hips widen as our cells rearrange themselves to accommodate new parts opening up. Widening of hips can indicate a settling into seat of wisdom from which we can widen our perspectives on things. It's a metaphoric throne in which we can relax and feel our inner power in a very literal way.

Even our hair turning different shades of gray/silver represents our growing crown as silver represents wisdom in the symbolic world. We become silver-crowned queens, worthy of respect and gratitude. That is why Menopause could be defined as a going-within time, a going-under time, so we can feel safe and unharried as powerful changes within us make themselves known and work through us to a new state of being.

I like to imagine our wombs as tabernacles of dark, moist, silken folds of soft tissue. Nestled in this lush, fertile cave is a golden egg awaiting fertilization with just the right sperm. From that fateful meeting, egg becomes embryo, fetus, toddler, child, adolescent, adult, and elder if the full circle of ripening occurs.

Every month for thirty-plus years of women's lives, this egg, in deep and intimate relationship with the moon and her phases of waxing, full, waning, and disappearing for three days will be born, grow to ripeness and if not fertilized, shed its potential through our monthly menses and begin the cycle once again.

The changing rhythmic cycles of Nature help us understand the journey of our bodies as they, too, move from Spring, the birth of the golden egg into Summer, its ripening and cessation in Autumn, the season of endings.

It's common for women to experience increased sporadic blood flow before the complete cessation of monthly menses. This, too, has symbolic meaning beyond our rational and medical explanations. We turn to Autumn in Nature to see that this is a time when the greening is over. The vibrant prolific growth of Spring and Summer come to an end with the leaves beginning a metamorphosis of color. The once-green primal shapes just before dying and falling to the ground have one last hurrah, one last awe-inspiring, full-throttled dance as they turn the skies into a panorama of bold, brazen beauty and brilliance for just a brief period before they fall to the ground in full surrender.

Perhaps that's a way of looking at the powerful blasts of blood that pour through us as our lifetime supply is finally finished. Our bodies must get used to a natural cycle ending. When we think about the intrinsic wisdom and beauty of this cycle repeating itself since the beginning of time in every girl/woman, it leaves one in a state of awe. We Women are the Lifemakers, the ultimate power that creates and sustains the human species.

And it all happens in these bodies of ours. These bodies, oh my god, these bodies. We could live on our knees bowing and paying obeisance to these bodies, these magnificent creations— staggeringly alive with feeling, hearing, smelling, tasting, touching, imagining, thinking, dreaming, sleeping, stretching, moving, creating, breathing. And we are home in them, these marvelous containers of fingers, knees, collarbones, spleens, intestines—all enrobed in Black, Brown, Olive, Red, Yellow, White, and every variation of the above—skin. Nothing but grace and gorgeous, these bodies of ours.

In closing, I will admit that it's taken years of moments and long bouts of suffering in this earth body of mine to recognize and claim what was mine all the while—that I belong on this beloved earth among the stars and all the living beings that surround and support it.

Menopause opened my eyes and heart to the knowing and feeling that all of us are unconditionally loved by every breath of the

Universe in every second. We live in a radiant realm of change. It is imperceptible, subtle, dramatic, on-going, moment by moment. This change is endlessly accompanied with potential, opportunity, loss, and transformation.

The natural world that lies outside our human-made dwellings calls to us, summons us, pulls us toward it, to experience its bounty and its beauty in all the myriad forms and voices of its inhabitants. Lake Michigan was at my doorstep and I was deaf to her entreaties until a dog named Kaley heard her call. I answered the door.

"When we experience beauty, we feel called.
The Beautiful stirs passion and urgency in us
and calls us forth from aloneness
into the warmth and wonder
of an eternal embrace.:
~ John O'Donohue, author of "Divine Beauty"

Lake Michigan Musings

Tender

There's a tenderness to the earth and sky that I feel when I walk this path along Lake Michigan in early morning. Birds are in full concert, air is fresh, stars are tucked away, and morning light is soft. The lines that separate everything are blurry and more nuanced. It's the liminal period between sleeping and waking that is laced with magic.

Objects are just moving into their daytime places—before lipstick and blush, before the world becomes raucous and randy once more. We're brand-new again as we are with every dawn—like beings emerging from the womb of night when all of our senses are still delicate and dreamy.

The Sun rises so effortlessly, elegantly each day. No hurry, no fuss—just rising into his throne ever since the Earth was born. When Sun retires for the day, the Moon begins her ascent like the Grande dame of the sky. Sometimes she lingers in the day just to keep an eye on that old man Sun.

And then, an entourage of stars come forth so elegantly, as though they too need to take their place in the grand design of night sky. It's all a majestic, rhythmic, ancient dance that these heavenly bodies have been doing forever, and we, too, are part of it. Those ancient rhythms are alive in us when we notice and are awed by this skyscape.

Nature offers herself for our pleasure, our reflection, our learning. She teaches us to let go gracefully of whatever we're holding onto when it isn't serving us or the world around us. She teaches us to live joyfully and whole-heartedly, to die quietly, respectfully; to be present to wherever we are and whom we are with.

For everything in life is temporary, including us. The best lesson of all for me is how to embrace and enjoy Beauty in all its myriad forms. Simple. Complex. Delicate. Intricate. Hidden. Apparent. Mysterious. Dangerous. That's what each day offers.

Intimacy

Intimacy. A word so human-centered, as though we can only be heart and soul close to another person like ourselves. As I walk on the bank above the Lake and down the hill toward her, I hear her call from the swish of her skirts along the shore; compelling, beckoning me to come closer, to walk beside her, to feel her vitality, all around me, within me. It's a call to intimacy and I respond gladly, willingly.

When I look out at the horizon, I can see the curve of the sky hovering over this magnificent body of water. The sun is there with a few fast-moving clouds. We're all together in this picture, this puzzle, this mystery of birds, trees, grasses, rocks, stones boats, bridges. Each has a separate life, and, yet we're all in this experience together. All of us breathe the same breath, feel the warmth of the same sun, and share in the same life energy, but in different ways and shapes.

As I walked home yesterday, I passed a yard with a rose bush in full bloom. I pressed my face into one of the flower faces to give my nostrils a lavish, unexpected treat. Beauty offers itself to us, through this panorama of nature that envelopes and accompanies us on our life journeys. That rose pulled me to itself. It needed to be noticed and admired as much as I needed to notice and admire it. It was an honest exchange, a quid pro quo, something for something. What good is poetry without a voice to sail upon?

Susan Winecki

So it is with Lake Michigan. I can admire her from afar yet she only becomes truly alive when I come closer, sometimes right to her delicate edge, the edge where the wet of her meets the dry of me and touches. When some part of her makes contact with some part of me, something new is shared between us. My own wild blue wetness is awakened in these moments and there is an intimacy between us that is precious and real.

Masterpiece

As I walk, I think about Lake Michigan and the fact that we have her here in our midst three hundred sixty-five days of every year. A masterpiece, a living work of art, ever-changing and drop-dead gorgeous. People wait in long lines and pay money to spend time in art galleries, museums to gaze at and admire famous works of art, shielded by glass plates and expensive high-tech security systems.

Lake Michigan is unguarded, unrestrained, free to the public. We are spoiled by beauty. We can walk past the ancient masterpiece of Lake Michigan with hardly a glance. That is what I did for a very long time before I began to wake up to her charms.

We don't tend to value what is free. But surely this Lake is a blessing. The knowing and feeling that we can access some part of ourselves that comes alive in her presence would be worth the price of admission for me in any event.

Alas, we have become a nation of consumers, drawn irresistibly to the almost magical attributes of technological wonders, including computers, TVs, digital phones, etc. They have transformed our lives in tremendous ways, and yet, and yet, there remains the magic, the wonder of this earth and sky holding us, breathing us, awaiting us. We can turn on our machines and behold the beauty of the natural world in its myriad forms and faces on the screen in front of us, but it's not the real thing.

The real thing is touching, stepping onto the living earth, feeling its quiet power beneath our soles, looking out at the cloud formations grazing the sky, listening to the inhales and exhales of the waves as they waltz onto the shore. It's the aliveness, the voluptuousness of this natural world that has no equal, no comparison, no competition in the human-made world. And it's always available for participating in. Just step outside.

"Stay near the beauty, for she will always strengthen you. She will bring your mouth close to hers and breathe—inspire you the way light does to the fields."
~ St. Thomas Aquinas

Wingspread

My walks beside the Lake feel separate and alien to my in-house life. When I walk outside by Lake Michigan, I'm entering another reality, another world. It's a reality I require now in my life and cherish. I can spread my wings out, here under this vast canopy of sky across the wide dance floor of the Lake.

In my house, this lavish sense of freedom is tucked away. Here, unbridled, I can take off, "fly into and out of clouds." I don't worry about what to wear, what to eat, whom to talk to, what to say. I drop all of those "what to's" at take-off and simply soar and spin through and in and out of this magic.

The freedom of the Lake and sky to be all of themselves all of the time gives me permission to be all of myself in their presence. And I don't need anyone's approval. I have spent so much of my life energy seeking approval from different and often, unhealthy sources. But here I am: part of creation. What more approval can there be for me, or any of us?

I love knowing that, and often forget it when my wings are tucked away in my in-house self. The Lake and sky only welcome and embrace. The idea that anyone of us can be rejected or diminished by another one of our own species is so absurd, so foreign to nature; yet it happens all the time in the human realm. We must find places where we receive unconditional love. Where we are urged to spread our wings, spread our joy and freedom all over the waiting earth and into the endless sky.

It's fun to think about getting my imaginary wings ready for take-off, as I lace up my walking shoes and head for the exit door.

"Dear God, please reveal to us your sublime beauty that is everywhere, everywhere, so that we will never again feel fright-ened. My divine love, my love, please let us touch your face."

~ Rumi

Enough

Walking along the Lake with sky all around me, I see that Lake and Sky have enough room in which to be themselves. I want to feel that I do also. The rooms I poke around in at home could be more but they are enough for me and my things in which to rest and feel settled. Inside my body are all the amazing organisms and living parts that have enough room for themselves to move around in and be healthy. My mind has enough room for my thoughts, ideas, and imaginings. My heart has enough room for love, tears, kindness, forgiveness, and beauty. There is room enough outside and room enough inside so appreciation and happiness can grow bigger and deeper each day that I am here.

And it isn't just about enough room to be oneself in, it's about enoughness itself.

That who I am and where I am in my life at any given time and place is enough.

I experience that from spending time with Lake Michigan. She is a body of liquid beauty that expresses herself through colors, textures, sounds, movements, conditions. How could there be any more of her than already exists? How could there be any more to sky or sun than there is?

They are enough. I am enough. All of us are enough, but that doesn't mean we can't open up new parts of ourselves and let other parts go. It simply means we can accept and come into deeper friendship with who we are at any moment, recognizing that we contain multitudes, as Walt Whitman, the poet, said. We have finite time on this beloved earth home, yet there are infinite possibilities for us to learn new dance steps while we're here.

If we pair the concepts of "enough" and "gratitude," we're in good company. Each offers the opportunity for a sense of inner quiet which we never seem to get our fill of in our lives.

Debut

Beauty is my caffeine. Give me the sky with an eyeful of Lake Michigan, a face full of fresh air, and I'm rarin' to go. It's the drama that's addictive. Like this morning, for instance: I left the house for my walk along the Lake and was taken captive by a fierce wind. It was frenzied, wild, whipping around, pushing and pulling everything in its path toward the southeast. The waves, like runners in a marathon race close to the finish line, pitched forward with their whole might.

I, too, was in the race, not knowing what the wind was pushing me toward. I kept pace with the waves and moved so rapidly I could feel the long bones in my legs making contact with the inside of my skin. Even my breathlessness didn't slow me down. Something was happening and I was in the whip of it. Suddenly, the waves and I came to a bend in the path, and I saw what the excitement was about.

The Sun, hidden behind this screen of dove gray and white billowy clouds, created a soft spray of silvered light to spread out from beneath the lower ledge of the cloud cover. Waves and wind crashed into each other, causing them to leap up and fall back into the foamy sea of Lake. They were like spectators at the finish of the marathon, trying to be first to witness the finale. The feeling of a palpable sense of anticipation in the elements surrounded me.

I turned my gaze toward the sky and the bristling water as the Sun began his ascent toward his throne in sky. The clouds parted slowly and made way for that rising fireball. Slowly, ever so slowly, he rose, resplendent in diamond-spun robes that fell in his wake and floated on the surface of the water.

All became quiet. The waves softened and moved toward the shore where I, transfixed, stood. The Sun King had risen and a new day was born.

I see now what the drama was about: the Sun was rising, and we had to make haste to be there on time for his morning debut.

Blue

The Lake and sky melted into one another this morning, with a blue so intensely alive, I could take my finger and make a smear across my cheek. And here I am, wearing my pallid winter white skin, walking under this blazing blue canopy, wishing I, too, were the color blue.

I breathed in the luscious morning air that enveloped me and thought about the variation in skin colors of humans. Animals, tree, insects didn't seem to harbor the biases against others of their kind that wore different shades of a common color. What does it matter anyway? I'd gladly wear the color of this sky if I had the choice.

As my legs and toes head south, stretching across the shore's veranda along the Lake, I know that the more time I spend in nature, the less judgmental and constricted I feel—mentally, emotionally, and physically. All of me benefits from this precious time, every time. I look down on the path I'm walking and notice a variety of multicolored rocks, stones, and twigs strewn about the earth.

Nature has endless freedom with which to express creativity and difference. The Lake, for instance, isn't limited to one color, texture, mood, or style. Her range of expressions is infinite according to the range of conditions she's engaged in at any given moment.

It's the same with the sky, exhibiting colors and patterns depending on a host of factors that determine the outcome.

Nature is not limited by our descriptions or categories. In contrast, we have a narrow range of approval ratings by and from one another. We live in very cramped quarters compared to the voluptuous variety of natural beings to which we are akin.

My mind notices and wonders these things as I walk in utter freedom and silence under this vast womb of sky, listening to the myriad calls and whistles of flying creatures.

Sky

The newly fallen autumn leaves crackle beneath my shoes as my legs lean long into the well-worn path along the shore. It is mine alone this Sunday morning. I am enrobed from head to foot in soft pallid sky. No sun today, just sky, the emptiness and roominess of naked sky. There's room to ramble in, room for my eyes to roam about without bumping into anything.

Sky has nothing to limit or confine it. It is endless and forever as I stand on the shore and gaze into it. I see the city's contour, the horizon where water and sky couple with room all around them for flying creatures.

Silver-winged planes fly through the sky around the curved globe of earth. West Indies, Africa, Minneapolis, who knows where they're headed.

There's room for fireworks, for billowy clouds to come together and pull apart, for smoke-colored clouds to drench the earth. There's room for spitting lightning and bellowing thunder, for wind to wreak havoc on settled places. There's room for hanging stars, spinning planets, for the silver moon to rise in blackness and stay all the next day if she wants to. There's room for hoofs and beaks and claws and tails and wings and song and moan and screech and howl, for liars and lovers, for mystics and murderers, for babies and elders and time for one to grow into the other.

Maples and oaks spread their branches wide over the sky prairies, willows spill like emerald waterfalls. There's room for the quiet unfolding and ripening of things.

I can poke around in myself here. I can fill the vastness with the stuff of my imagination. The sky is generous and inviting. It will carry my dreams to faraway places my body may not get to. That's the pleasure of dreaming.

Stillness

On this late April day, we earth beings can't wait for the Sun to finally settle in and take his place in the vast sea of sky. But Sun is hidden. Lake is quiet. Trees stand motionless, and birds are nowhere to be heard. It's almost eerie in a way, walking along the Lake in this stillness. Walking here, I am so aware of how everything is so temporary, impermanent. There's grace in that awareness along with a degree of uncertainty.

If everything is temporary, that means me too. I am only here for a finite time. How many generations of humans and non-human life have been sunned, housed, and quenched by this Sun, Lake and Earth?

Once again, I am stunned at the mystery of this small yet expansive world I live in. There is no end to the endless questions and wonderings of it all. I just know that I love this Lake and sky and all the beauty that sustains and nourishes me each moment of my life. If only I could remember to remember more often and to say thank you more often for the miracle of this wisdom and benevolence that holds me in its embrace.

It's way too easy to get caught up in my own sense of importance and forget that I, too, carry an expiration date. For now, I'm enjoying the stillness of beauty. If I can keep that memory alive in myself, death will have no power over me. I'll just return to where I came from. Maybe. Who knows? Who can say?

Diamonds

Lake Michigan has pulled all the stars from the night sky into her lap this morning as she glitters and glamours past me. She wears a cape of shimmering silver like a royal robe on the surface of her waves and the sun king hovers, keeping a captivated eye on her. I think we are hot-wired for beauty—to see it, feel it, hear it, taste it, touch it. It humanizes us, spiritualizes us, opens our hearts to our own inner beauty and relationship with each other.

Nature has no self-consciousness, restraint, or limit to expressing its beauty. An orchid pours forth every millimeter of its tiny radiant body into open space. Trees reach high into the heavens and deep into the earth. We live among billions of beauty beings and yet we seem to be the only ones who hold back, who cling to our illusions of safety and envy other humans who dare to reveal more of themselves.

Where did we miss the turn into the arms of Nature? What happened to our deep soul and spirit longing to explore the wild body of earth on whom our very lives depend? Many of us can't relate to a sense of beauty lurking in the deep darkness within us, but sometimes a dream, an epiphany, a thought, a memory awakens us momentarily into something other than what we know. We are summoned in those transient moments to a seeing, a deeper familiarity, mysterious and marvelous. It's like a homecoming, those moments when we feel we belong here, we are safe here, we are loved here.

Friend

Lake Michigan became a great source of comfort and support for me when I received the news of a dear, dear friend's death. I was inconsolable for a time, yet I kept up my walks beside her. This death was unexpected, sudden, and I reacted with intense shock and denial. I knew from my own and other's experience in dealing with loss of this magnitude that the initial turning away from this news can be temporarily helpful in buying a little time in which to get used to a death.

I was grateful for that time.

Walking, walking, walking through my tears alongside Lake M. moved me forward in my grieving and grounded me. The earth was mighty below me, the sky was constant above me, and the Lake held her beauty and grace beside me. They were all balm for the soreness of my soul and spirit.

There was something especially soothing about being in the presence of water when I was so very vulnerable and emotionally naked. Water doesn't confront, it merely companions and compassions.

That's how it felt walking this trail of sadness: that I was in the best of hearts even though they weren't human.

Susan Winecki

It is a blessing to be able to find refuge in a time of deep sadness. A place to go to that's welcoming and quiet without expectations or questions. I could retreat there for as long as I needed.

Lake Michigan offered me a respite that was hard to find in my too-busy world. She is friend and family in a different form and just what I needed for my tender heart.

Wicked

The wind was wicked today, pushing against me, biting my cheeks with its sharpness, creating havoc in the order of things. I struggled to walk upright as the wind drove the Lake's swollen waters into spikes of foamy white that crashed into the offshore boulders.

This was a battle—not a casual, easy stroll along the Lake as I braved through every step. One of the joys and challenges of walking this path in every kind of weather is being able to experience every kind of weather and know that all these elements alone and in communion with each other are constantly changing, moving in a rhythm of their own.

By the time I'm finished with this writing, the weather will be another way. I know the wind's sweetness on those days when it moves softly over my skin and through my hair. I know its playfulness when it tips my hat from my head and sends it flying. It can be quiet or soaring, it can unforgiving, destructive, or tenacious.

I know wind inside of me, too, when that feeling of restlessness is churning up inside of me and I can't settle down. It's like an inner wind is blowing through my comfort zones, causing all sorts of unsettledness inside.

And I know that this state inside me is only temporary. It will quiet down at some point and let me be. Even that state, too, is only temporary. Everything alive is in movement all the time, whether or not we are aware of it. It's reassuring to know that and be grateful for its temporariness.

Silver

This is a day of grey. Lake and sky have colluded to create a somber grey sea and skyscape. It's often hard to find beauty in grey, especially in the changing hilltops of our bodies.

I'm of course referring to our hair as it moves into its aging phase. We notice and admire nature's gifts when they pour forth their spring and summer beauty in extravagant colors and textures. We are enticed by their fecundity and forthrightness.

But it doesn't last. It can't last.

I was enchanted by clusters of fiery red tulips as I walked past the other day. Now, several days later, they look tattered and torn, the petals dropping to the waiting earth to catch them as they fall.

My once deep brunette treetop tresses are now turning grey gradually, effortlessly.

I haven't been consulted about this alteration, so I've decided to reframe this transformation to grey into a more suitable word: silver. In the sun's or moon's light, that grey streak could look like silver.

In alchemy, silver is the feminine element and gold the masculine. I just decided that I'm growing my silver crown as I'm aging. Silver also represents wisdom in many indigenous cultures. I'll tuck that into my reframe also.

Susan Winecki

Grey is just one piece of the panorama gracing my eyes as I walk. Alongside it are green grasses and the long swinging arms of green-laced branches where multi-colored, feathered singing creatures flit from stage to stage crooning their hearts out.

I'm once again walking in beauty and kindness. Why not think about wearing kindness on a grey day, and maybe the world will see it through a silver lens.

That's the benefit of reframing. We can always look at things from a different perspective, especially when it turns the picture into pleasure.

Alone

I walked along the Lake this morning and kept pace with waves like rollerblades gliding across its wet floor with a casual wind as an assist. A day easy to be in. A day to be quiet and alone in.

Beauty and solitude. That's a good marriage. There's something lovely about not having to pay attention to another person—just being in the company of nature that unconditionally accepts and welcomes.

Beauty waits for us to discover her. She's patient. I find her most often when I am alone as I walk, watch, listen, and open myself up to what's right here, now. There's nowhere to hide from myself out here. I must be totally present and vulnerable, open to whatever makes itself visible and heard.

It is like being in a state of nobody-ness until I must become somebody again and take my place in the world of affairs that lie outside this quiet realm. But this separation of inside and outside is just a way of forgetting that we're always enveloped and held in this natural world.

I can be looking out the window of a tall building and see treetops, sunshine, or clouds moving through the sky's runway.

I pass by a stand of trees in various sizes and shapes. They remind me of ballet dancers in their various postures and poses, so graceful and strong, their outstretched branches reaching way up high in the sky, greedy for the sun's golden to green them.

Susan Winecki

There's always something to savor out here, something to notice and be glad about. Noticing is the key for me. And I notice that I observe best when I'm alone, and open to the generosity and graciousness of this landscape.

Grandmother

Lake Michigan never disappoints or fails to enchant me as I walk beside her. Like a gracious grandmother, she welcomes and makes a place for me to dawdle and dream as I walk alongside her.

Human grandmothers tend to the body and spirit. Lake Michigan tends to the soul. I come here for my daily fix. In the quiet bliss of dawn, my senses come alive and extend like hungry tentacles to the natural world around me. My skin loves the wet cold pecks of still-falling snow alighting on it, like ballet dancers. Legs and lungs find their tempo and move rhythmically with each other, following the path that leads me along a long slice of winter beauty.

It's reassuring being out here. A sense of order and clarity is ever-present. All my inner disarray and confusion seem to shift and move into places within me more comfortable and less troublesome. My restlessness subsides, my heart purrs a little, and my senses are more alert, yet relaxed.

Maybe it's because everything in nature is where it's supposed to be. There is great comfort in this natural arrangement of life outdoors. I remind myself to whisper a thank you to all the non-human companions that live and thrive here, far away from the madding and maddening crowds.

As I walk up the hill toward my house, I hear the cars speeding by and plane overhead! But the sky and sea of Lake continue being themselves regardless of the noise. They have no clock to punch, no one standing over them watching and judging their comings and goings. If the sun wants to take a day off to play hide and seek with the clouds, who can stop him? If the clouds want to spend the day making art in the sky, they can too.

But not today. No one is out playing today. The clouds have banded together and lay leaden across the Lake as I take one last look. They will be here in another arrangement before long and it, too, will be temporary.

Just like us.

Dancing

Lake Michigan is dancing this morning. A low-lying sheet of striated grey cloud hovers close to her, but she is unfazed by it. A blue sky arches above the cloud blanket with just enough sunlight that sneaks through and turns the surface of the waves into glimmering white-silver.

I find it challenging to stay focused on any one feature of the Lake as she's constantly, rhythmically in motion. Today, the waves leap and lunge northward toward the land-earth boundary that stops their gait. Her expression is ever-changing. The clouds now move down upon the Lake and cover her with their greyness.

The Lake's edges are lined by the naked limbs of tall trees on this December morning. Lullabyed and rocked into tranquility by a soft wind, the trees know the songs of waves caressing the shore. How lovely to be a tree along Lake Michigan's shoreline, a tree charmed by bird wings, wind currents, and human murmurings.

A gull glides through the air and fish slide through the liquid womb of the Lake. I would love to be that grace-filled and nimble, in delicious harmony with wind currents that change, charge, increase and drop into partnership with the Lake, whose very essence is change.

Weather

I like the moody, unpredictable, always-changing weather of the Midwest. Today as I walk, the sky is overcast and the Lake is quiet. It wears the sky's greyness.

Yesterday, sunlight filled every corner. People were out in noisy multiples, walking, biking, motorcycling, driving. The weather in the Midwest challenges us. People tend to complain and focus on an atmosphere that feels oppressive, even negative. Grey days can feel especially unrelenting.

But before long, it's another way. Many people need, want or thrive on being showered daily with the sun's golden rays. Held captive to successive days of grey Winter weather can lead one to understand the need for change. Maintaining an attitude of inner sunniness day in and day out can be difficult considering the challenges that life confronts us with on a regular basis.

Grey days can test my own patience, endurance and ability to feel good inside while the weather outside deprives me of needed uplift and affirmation.

Perhaps the weather is an apt metaphor for our personal mood changes. It could help us learn how to strengthen our own inner weather patterns and remember that this mood or feeling is only temporary. It will pass.

Artistry

I'm here again, walking into another splendid Lake Michigan morning. Her artistry entices and infuses me, so I, too, become part of her palette. The gulls chase each other as I watch them dive and shriek with glee in the vast playground of sky. I stop, startled, as a red-tailed fox walks by as though I were just an old stump of tree.

What company is mine on these daily sojourns! It's another new slice of day brimming with figures and shapes that breathe in the same beauty as I do.

On another morning, I passed by a coyote who apparently crossed the road from Seminary Woods toward the lakeshore. He sat still on a leaf-covered hill, looking somewhere off in the distance. I wondered if he was lonely, looking for one of his own kind to look back at him. I whispered hello silently and kept moving. He's remained with me in thought and imagining.

Was there a time when I was coyote, when I was a daring, darting seagull, a lumbering porcupine hiding somewhere in this old forest, now an overgrown hill by the shore?

As always, I'm delighted that every time I enter this quiet Eden, its beauty never repeats or gets tired of itself. It's hidden and even obvious gems glitter a different way, show light in a new shade and reveal secret hiding places and nests of our local non-human residents.

I feel a kind of reverence being here. When I was a girl crossing the threshold into the grand entrance of my Catholic Church, I felt its beauty and spaciousness as a refuge from my too-small house with no privacy or stillness. It was a place of safety and grandeur, both nourishing, holding me closely.

This path, this walk, is that to me. I am young here, fresh, full of dreams and desires that ooze forth freely. They make their way into the clouds, into the sun's glance, for a little while each time.

Arrival

The air out here feels heavy and slow and moving as I follow my path along the shore. My legs work, my arms swing, my heart beats, my lungs breathe, but it feels like the energy out here is holding its breath, holding all of us in stillness. I can hear the birds chirping a song of cheer to the dreary Lake and sky.

And best of all, even though the day is grim with grayness, I come to an open field alongside the Lake where the grass is brilliant with greenness and peppered all over with sunbursts of blooming dandelions, erect like miniature soldiers. No sun above, but thousands of tiny suns all over the green earth. They were proud and willing to brighten the day bereft of the sun's rays.

I am reminded of how each day gives birth to another version of itself and how we tend to count our lives in days and put frames around those we consider special or precious. Someone some-where is celebrating a birthday, or remembering with sadness the loss of a beloved.

I can feel the sky readying itself for a good sob, dark clouds gathering above me. Then I gaze once again at the dandelions and know that regardless of the weather outside, we can still create magic wherever we place or find ourselves on any given day. We don't need the sun in order to give a smile or a hug to someone.

Susan Winecki

We don't need the soft wind to caress our cheeks in order to wave hello to a friend or give a stroke of delight to our animal companion. We can bring beauty to whatever kind of day, just like the dandelions spreading their beauty across the earth under a forlorn sky.

Lesson

I want to be more like the recklessly alive, swift-moving, yet rhythmic and energetic Lake Michigan. This morning, she reminds me of a polka dance, the musicians singing and playing with joyous abandonment. The tassels of the silver-tipped waves fly through the air like young girls braids as their partners twirl them around and around in mad gay circles. Even the feeding birds alighted on this raucous dance floor are caught up in the energy. I'm jealous as I stand quietly watching the waves come whirling before me, only to crash loudly on the rocky shore and hurry back for more.

I reflected on my own life and wondered when I last felt wild and free as Lake Michigan this morning. She has boundaries, limits all around her but that doesn't prevent her from the joyous abandonment she exhibits in these moments I am witnessing.

Abandonment often means to me the experience of a loss, a broken heart or a leaving of a precious person in our lives. I like the Lake's expression of abandonment better. These waves of energy pouring themselves out under the sky, unteathered, unapologetic.

The birds get it, the boughs lying close to the shore get it as their multi-layered leaves shimmy in accompaniment. I'm the only one now sitting perched on a quiet rock watching all this merriment in action.

Susan Winecki

Now my time for musing is ending as the polka-dancing waves quiet down and become a waltz. Who knows? Maybe tomorrow when I come, I'll be lucky enough to catch the sounds and rhythm of a new dance!

Quiet

The Lake wore repose this morning as though she were shrouded in a soft blue-grey shawl of finely woven cotton. Her utterly still surface lay trancelike for as far as my eyes could see; the surround of the city hardly discernable as it stood behind her like a fortress.

The edges of the water lining the shore reminded me of Belgian lace, samples of which are sometimes found in antique clothing stores attached to necklines of expensive dresses and lingerie. It is as though spiders had woven it instead of human hands. Even the sun seemed to just barely rest on her.

A pair of geese glided in front of me to join their larger party way out in the distance. There was an overall sense of reverence that emanated from the quiet pond beside me as if the Lake were in a state of deep meditation, not to be disturbed.

For some strange reason, the Lake in her state of repose reminded me of my father's face as he lay in repose in his final resting place. My family and I marveled at how youthful and at peace he looked. When I mentioned this to the funeral director, he said it was not an uncommon phenomenon.

We carry much tension and stress in our faces and bodies. When the lines disappear, our skin reflects inner peace and tranquility. We were all grateful that my dad was finally at peace and he gave us all the gift of seeing him that way.

Susan Winecki

I think it's helpful for charging-ahead humans to have positive images of repose and peacefulness. We are so often in states of serious stimulation, frantic, hurried movement and tension.

Once the day gets ahold of us, it becomes almost impossible to put the brakes on and slow down for any length of time. We need to let nature be our balm, our role model for feeling less anxious and more fluid.

Wild

A roaring, snorting wind pounded at my house through the night, making me wary of walking out this morning. With layered clothing and hunched shoulders, I stepped into dawn, happy to find a more timid version of last night's stallion kicking up its heels.

This morning's wind even felt like good company as it accompanied me down my usual path along the Lake, prodding me along with its jaunty lifts and swirls. The scattered, torn tree branches and shoreline debris were everywhere. I have to thread carefully through the remnants of last night's free-for-all.

I turn my disconsolate gaze from the strewn-filled path as her waves whip and whistle over the break wall and turn summersaults onto the highest rock ledges. Just try and tame that wild sea of Lake.

I'm reminded of messages so often given to girls at a young age about learning to be modest, quiet, and obedient in the presence of adults.

Lake Michigan spits in the face of all those admonitions. She's a feminine element who is free, haughty, and thousands of years old. She's beholden to no one and belongs grandly, gloriously, and fiercely to herself. She's an example in the natural world worth emulating. It's so easy to get caught up in social approval, of behaving in ways that will make others comfortable, often at our own expense. It's important to be true to our real selves in a myriad of expressions; to be kind to others at the same time.

Not always easy, but worth practicing.

Stonestill

The Lake lay still as stone and smooth as glass this morning as I rested my just-awakening gaze upon her. The sun's light stretched long above her, as though he was lying on her gently, tenderly.

I feel myself softening as I walk alongside their beauty. It spreads across the rocky shore like fresh honey on a warm baking powder biscuit. I walk in quiet these autumn mornings. The morning chill keeps visitors scarce and I like it. The sun is readying himself for exit to warmer shores.

Already this morning, his caress is more detached, less intense than in the heat of summer. The sky seems to lower itself also as the sun prepares for leaving to keep the Lake from being totally abandoned and forlorn with her lover's departure. We all have to adjust to winter's coming and it's comforting to know that we are among friends when we step outside.

I feel different inside when I am in the company of nature. My mind is less restless, my heart quiets, and there's a sense of alert aliveness that comes over me.

Maybe that's because everything in the natural world is where it's supposed to be.

The sky is in its place, the Lake is in her place, the sun, birds, clouds, shoreline, trees, and skyline are all where they are supposed to be, doing what they are supposed to do. There is comfort in that, especially when I am in a state of disarray about my own affairs.

I remind myself when I'm wandering through this cathedral of majesty to say thank you to the non-human companions that live and thrive here. That's why I selfishly love it when summer's fire turns cold and dreary, when the sky moves in closer, when the birds fly south, when the grasses turn oatmeal-colored, when the trees shed their summer tresses and everything in this temperate climate just gets down to its nubs.

It's beautiful in a different way.

Solitude

I walk softly in this lush landscape of burgeoning nature. It's a lavish sensory feast to be out here in the presence of Lake, sky and earth with their generosity pouring itself out everywhere. They offer us endless gifts and today I take them into myself with gratitude and gladness.

It's always about beauty; today it's about solitude. There's something easy about not having to pay attention to another person beside me. Others are on the path in their own personal landscapes.

It's in these early-morning walks that I feel the Lake's bounty so brazenly.

I pass a lone woman sitting on a makeshift seat along the shore. She looks out as I do at the close and yet faraway beauty whipping around her. I wonder what she's thinking and feeling as she sits in repose, surrounded by the wildness of the Lake. I wonder if she too would love to feel that sense of freedom and daring that the Lake is exhibiting. A devil-may-care attitude. How delicious to get out on a dance floor and just let it rip.

I think about the myriad creatures and lifeforms living in the belly of the Lake, what it must be like to move about in liquid freedom. The sky creatures and the water creatures both share this reality of boundlessness. No wonder they move with a lyric grace and agility.

Susan Winecki

We human creatures have much to learn and admire in other forms of life. That's the giftedness of Nature's expression, and we live in relationship with these different beings. We can observe and appreciate their giftedness to us. The lone woman has alighted now and moves slowly away from her park perch. Meanwhile, the rest of the day is beckoning me also to return to my home perch.

Beckoning

The Lake is held captive this morning by a dreary grey, oppressive sky lying heavily upon her slow-moving waters. I want to go out and push it away so she can purr and pulsate once again.

Eight inches of still falling, moisture-laden snow have piled up over the last twelve hours, transforming the bald winter landscape into a voluptuous one. The contrast between the looming grey of the sky and water against the whiteness of the snow is stunning.

The brown, crusty beach is covered with snow that looks like layers of thin white tissue paper, the kind used in wrapping expensive gifts before boxing up. The waves that thud onto the shore are swollen and heavy with the weight of the snow and sky upon them.

Lake Michigan never disappoints. She welcomes the company of all the earth's creatures to take their place both inside and outside of her. My legs and lungs have found their tempo and fall more easily into the footprints on the path that brought me here this morning.

I'm aware of a sound that's strange, chilling somehow but beckoning. My curiosity is aroused as I try to find where the mysterious, enticing sound is. The wind is absent and the sound carries itself to where I stand like a tiny speck on this long beach with my ears widened. It feels somehow like I'm listening to the sound of eternity, the echo of primordial elements that existed before words came into being.

My imagination is on fire now and once more, I'm amazed at how a simple walk along the Lake in a new snowfall can take me to another world in a matter of footsteps.

I don't know what the eerie melody I'm hearing is or where it's coming from, but I love that it, too, accompanies me on this cheerless day just like the mighty Lake alongside of me.

Vanishing

Beauty, as a presence, can be a very momentary experience, so we must catch and hold it in those precious moments of joy it provides.

I think of sunrises and sunsets. The sun tenderly arises from its dark womb to grace us with its arrival. He's never in a hurry when he comes forth. So slowly, softly he enters, enveloped in swirls of color. Unlike many of us who wake up and run to ready ourselves for the day at hand.

Sundown also presents us with a humbling opportunity to both witness and participate in the leaving of the mighty Sun-King. No matter how many cars are moving through space, or how much noise emanates from the bustling metropolis, he majestically descends back into the darkening womb of earth.

There is privilege in awakening to the rising of the sun and witnessing its leaving. I can feel that tenderness when I arise early. The birds are alive in full concert, calling to one another across the empty space. It's that sacred time when the Lake and all of nature are shrouded in elusiveness and mystery. We're brand-new all over again.

The Dream-maker has retired for the day, leaving us in a state of readiness and renewal as the day unwinds itself within and without us. Everything seems delicate to the touch in these dawns and declines of the light, especially our senses which come alive in the presence of beauty.

I feel myself as brand-new also and not to move too quickly or mindlessly. I always think there could be bleachers set up in opportune places to watch the Sun rise and descend. We could bow in gratitude for the spectacle of beauty the Sun provides us with each morning and evening.

Generosity

As I strode silently and slowly on my well-traveled Lake path, I thought about nature's generosity, especially Lake Michigan's. She's always here—in beauty, kindness, silence, and companionship. I can walk to her side or sit on the earth beneath a tree to catch a glimpse of her shimmering in the foreground as her waves call hello to all of us looking her way.

She is constant, contained and forthright. I come to her when I'm wracked with indecision or some hard-to-deal-with human difficulty and pour my broken words into her wide-open-heartedness. Then I feel lighter because I've given her the worries I brought and her waves carry them away.

I've become dependent on nature's generosity. There is no holding back from any of its gifts or living forms. When it's blooming time, in the plant Queendom, it gives power and strength to the newly arriving and we receive the benefits of its generosity. Nature's bounty is boundless, no strings attached.

There's only one expectation in return, and that is respect, love, and protection. That's a fair quid pro quo for all of us to be welcomed at the table of nature's plenty. No one is turned away. The table is always set for as many guests as show up. Just bring a big appetite and be prepared to dine lavishly on the gifts that will envelope you in this natural world. Free. No charge.

Susan Winecki

So much of what I've learned and continue to learn about becoming a human being comes from spending time in the natural world. It's brimming with subtle but rich teachings about the momentariness of life, its unpredictability, its harshness at times, its constant change, the ever-present state of decay, death and rebirth, and best of all, its beauty, mystery, and magnanimity.

Spider-Webbed Fence

I walked along a spider-webbed fence this morning for perhaps a mile. It was a dull-green painted metal fence with round bars built to protect the expensive large boats docked on the Lake side of it.

A ferocious thunderstorm roared through the night, pouring huge deposits of water upon the earth along with pockets and puddles of rainwater remnants underfoot. Sun was already in place when I noticed a dazzling parade of spiderwebs spread between the sturdy round fence poles. Myriad shapes, sizes, and textures adorned this metal canvas.

There must have been many dozens of webs, all in some kind of intimate relationship with one another. Sun was hitting the delicate strands. Tiny droplets of water clung to them glistening. Every web was diamond-studded, as though it had been spun by fairies at dawn once the rain rested.

And they went on and on, some larger webs with several smaller ones attached to its lower arms. Each was unique in its presentation and design, left there for passersby to stop and ponder them with awe and delight.

The next morning, I walked along the same fence. The webs were gone—not a trace of their gift remains, only my remembering. That's the thing about nature. You never know what you're going to run into when you're in this wild space. It reminds me to stay alert and grounded at the same time.

Susan Winecki

Walking along Lake Michigan reminds me of being a diner at an elegant restaurant with everything in its right place at the right time in the right atmosphere. Everything ready of an exquisite dining experience. All I need to do is show up, sit down, relax and be prepared for a sumptuous, sensory meal.

That's how I think of entering the presence of Lake Michigan, like I'm arriving for a savory feast of the senses.

And of course, she's doesn't disappoint.

Reflection

The Lake is serene this morning, easy to be with, to walk beside. She asks nothing of me. I ask nothing of her. We're just spending time in each other's company. Looking up at the sky as I walk, blue with fleeting clouds; the sun soft and warm on my bare skin, I realize how patient nature is. However long it takes us to notice beauty enveloping us, it waits.

Nature has its own rhythms, its own seasons. The sun will rise majestically every day, whether or not I notice it. It will green and brown the earth from its deserts to the tundras when it's that part of the earth's time.

The moon will move in mystery from a thin crescent to radiant fullness and disappear for three days until it begins its monthly ritual once again.

The sky will remain sky in all its distant and remote unknowing-ness as it has for an eternity of years.

Like a vast womb, these elements are woven together in silent and natural beauty, holding us, awaiting us. The natural world that is home to us puts no pressure on us to change or notice its gifts.

And yet we know in some part of ourselves that it's an amazing experience to be alive in this ever-changing, enduring, patient, and eternally beneficent planet.

I look at myself in the mirror and see the face of a woman aging. I look into the mirror of sky and it looks the same as it did when I was a child, lying on my back counting the stars at night. The sun feels the same today as it did when I swam under its warm touch as an adolescent girl.

As I've traveled to different places in different seasons, the sun and sky are with me there also. I see the absolute order of the architecture, this natural arrangement of the elements providing for us the perfect conditions for our growth and ripening.

Everything in order, in balance, in harmony.

Life on the River

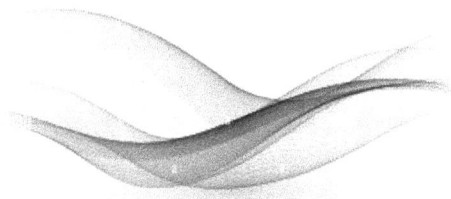

Moving

The move from Lake Michigan to the Milwaukee River was dramatic in unanticipated ways. I knew that my relationship with Lake Michigan was solid and unwavering, but I had no idea about the level of grief I would experience when I relocated.

My dad died some years ago, but my tears for his passing were slight compared to the tears I shed when I left the Lake. I had no idea that this rupture of space between us would create a loss in me so tender and acute.

I needed to be reminded that true heartfelt relationship, no matter what form of living being it comes in, brings pleasure as well as pain when it changes.

I discovered the beauty and power of the River after spending time in her presence and the following essay speaks to that.

River

I sit in the chilled breath of an October morning alongside the Milwaukee River. Her brown skin is wearing blue sky today. There are long-legged trees, barren and black-stemmed. One tree stands alone, dressed in morning sun, like golden honey melting down its long trunk, pooling into a shimmering circle on the river's face.

A soft wind caresses the serpentine movement of the water as it carries past me, like a funeral barge, the fallen foliage of the tall trees. I name the curled leaves as they float by: my mom, dad, grandparents, and others who've had their turn at being here. A steady flow of life beginning, ending, and returning.

River is old. She knows her way home, deep and wild. She knows the song of thunder, and wind, and moonless nights. She knows the heartbeat of the earth, the language of the standing, flying, feeding, singing, and paddling ones. All are welcome to feast and rest on her liquid lap. The river is a mirror for all the faces and forms reflected in her moving grace and grit, yet she remains mystery, belongs to herself and the earth. Just as we humans do.

When I walk alongside Lake Michigan, I am seized by her glamour. When I sit alongside the Milwaukee River, her brown-skinned beauty touches me more quietly, slowly. I must be still. Soon something begins to stir in me. I feel cradled and carried into her cadence, her rhythm. Then my breath deepens, my blood is more robust and yet all of me is calmer, easier, like caffeine and tranquilizer at the same time.

The River enervates and sedates, soothes and excites. Delight and danger travel along with her. The contrast between the Great Lake and the River startles and both carry her own brand of mystery and treasure. And each is here for us to cherish and protect. That's our part of the quid pro quo.

Welcome

We travel around the world to visit other countries and cultures for adventure, learning, curiosity, romance, change. But right here, we have this exotic world of nature. Nature is easily accessible for our coming to it. There is no cost, no language barriers. In fact, we don't need to speak at all. Our experience will ripen and deepen if we come to nature in silence, stillness, and wonder.

It's simply astounding what sights and sounds we experience when we take our seats among the many foreign and fascinating creatures that we live among. My closest neighbors include an egret, a red fox, coyotes, white-tailed deer, wild turkeys, a coterie of squirrels and woodpeckers of every species. The brown-skinned Milwaukee River in my backyard is home to an endless array of fish, turtles, ducks, birds, and rocks of every size and shape.

It seems like a strange idea to make friends with Nature and a river. They are in such different forms from us humans. Yet we make friends with dogs, cats and other mammal and plant beings and it doesn't seem unnatural at all.

Many of our non-human companions become intimate life companions because we've developed relationships with them. If we can do that with other non-human beings, why not be friends with a river? We're both alive, we're both story, and we each have a history and a home on the earth. We can't live without each other.

We need rivers. Rivers need our protection and maintenance. We need water to live. Who wouldn't want to be friends with a natural being so alive and interesting?

Closing

Lake Michigan midwifed me through this turbulent time of change in my life.

Daily morning walks into the just-awakening tender sky and Lake, enveloped in light as fragile as orchid petals ushered my crossing the threshold from parts of a dying self into a new self that was just forming.

The Lake, Rivers, Earth want us to enjoy their banquets. An orchestra doesn't want to play to an empty house, nor does Beauty. It wants us to fill our craving for happiness with its endless gifts.

Lakes and Rivers are like beautiful women who want to be seen, loved, and protected from harm. Save a chunk of yourself for Nature; a good-sized chunk so it will support and sustain your spirit and soul better than most relationships we give ourselves over to. A life-giving, enduring relationship is their offering.

Menopause is to be revered. It's not just hormonal, physical as we've been led to believe. It is a major opportunity for deep, self-affirming transformation. It carries soul lessons and we have to be willing to listen and to respond.

May your journey lead you to who you came here to be despite the constraints and corsets of a reality which fails to see and honor our amazing women selves. Be brave. Open up to your true warrior self and live in this glorious world at home in yourself.

A Tree I Love

Before we met, I strolled past you
on my walks along Lake Michigan. Now
I walk toward you in anticipation
 of leaning my forehead and hands onto your
beveled bark skin for just a few breaths
before I head home. You stand like a one
legged giant in this circle of space on the
corner where Memorial Lake and Lagoon drives
meet in Milwaukee's Lakefront.

You stand silent, unmoving. A sentinel overseeing
daily onslaughts of cars, motorcycles, exhaust
fumes, dog pee, sirens, blaring radios, people
paying no mind. But above the clamor below
you are upright, stretching long
between freedom and burial, your towering
headdress of sun-baked leaves forms a cathedral
of majesty.

Fall has come. Your singing leaves fall to
their fate. Bundled into plastic bags
heaved onto the backs of city trucks
driven off into unmarked graves.
Your long, bare, black arms rest and wait.
I come to you and rest my forehead
on your beveled bark skin and
wait with you.

~ Susan Winecki, Fall of 2020

www.ingramcontent.com/pod-product-compliance
Lightning Source LLC
Chambersburg PA
CBHW041923090426
42741CB00020B/3455